THE HOCUS-POCUS OF THE UNIVERSE

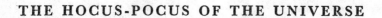

WINNER OF THE WALT WHITMAN AWARD FOR *1976*

*Sponsored by The Academy of American Poets
and supported by the Copernicus Society of America,
the Walt Whitman Award is given annually
to the winner of an open competition among American
poets who have not yet published their first
books of poetry.*
JUDGE FOR *1976:*   W I L L I A M   S T A F F O R D

The Hocus-Pocus

of the Universe

❧ *Laura Gilpin*

DOUBLEDAY & COMPANY, INC.
Garden City, New York 1977

Grateful acknowledgment is made to the editors of the following magazines
in which some of these poems first appeared, for permission to reprint:

"Dust," "Seeing a Dog in the Rain," "Souvenir" in *Chelsea* 32, August
1973, Copyright © 1973 by Chelsea Associates, Inc.; "The Mittens My
Grandmother Made," "A Fine Afternoon for Flying Kites," "Separation"
in *Hanging Loose*, No. 28, August 1976, Copyright © 1976 by *Hanging
Loose;* "The Two-headed Calf," "The Magi," "Coming Home" in
Transatlantic Review, Fall 1976, Copyright © 1976 by Transatlantic
Review, Inc.

ISBN: 0-385-11600-4 Trade
ISBN: 0-385-12215-2 Paperbound
Library of Congress Catalog Card Number 76-2746

To M. & D., with love

I would like to thank The Academy of American Poets and the Copernicus Society for making possible things that otherwise wouldn't be. And special thanks to Jane Cooper, Beth Straus, and Muriel Dunn.

L.C.G.

The universe . . . is a configuration of people, places, and things . . . held together by the same mysterious energy that keeps atoms together in the same molecule.

T. H. GRIFFIN

Contents

I

II

IV

III

THE HOCUS-POCUS OF THE UNIVERSE

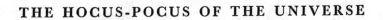

 *I*

The Meaning

You find yourself among
blind artists and deaf musicians
where the landscape is colorless
and music has only one note like a moan.

Singers without voices
are practicing the scales of silence
sculptors without hands
are licking the stone.

Your heart in its tower of bones
is tolling but no one can hear.

You tell yourself you don't belong here
you have no reason to stay.

But on the morning you planned to leave
you discover that your feet are gone
your legs end below the knees.

Suddenly you understand
your purpose in life:
to crawl through the ferns and mushrooms
asking why.

Spring

(for Aggie)

Very early every morning
my great-aunt, still in her
bathrobe and bedroom slippers,
goes out into the yard
to see the flowers.

Slowly, taking great care
with each step, she walks first
to the row of azaleas by the fence
stopping for a long time
at each one,

then to the camellias
which are almost gone
where she brushes away
the dead flowers, then
to the dogwood where

she pulls away several strands
of Spanish moss, then
to the wisteria where she
leans down to smell them,
then to the pear tree,

then to the lily bed,
to the hydrangeas, to
the magnolia fuscata
where the petals fall
loosely into her hand.

And then she stops and
looking back over all of them
she nods. Finally she turns
and begins the long walk
back towards the house.

And when she sits quietly in
the rocking chair by the window,
the hem of her bathrobe
is still wet with dew.

The Mittens My Grandmother Made

My grandmother made me some mittens
knowing I like them better than gloves,
knowing I like the way all four fingers
keep each other warm, the way
they can huddle together into a fist
and the isolated thumb
abandoning his own sweater
to join the rest of the crowd.

And as I wear these mittens
I think of my grandmother,
her hands working like cricket legs all night
and the rocking chair thumping like a dog's tail,
and I think of my grandmother, thinking of me
trudging through the winter,
bundled up like a bear,
my feet buried in eskimo boots
and my hands in her mittens.

Overlooking the Hospital Garden

You had decided for me
Long before I was born:
    I was going to be a girl,
    I was going to be the apple of your eye.

And you were there
When the nurses brought me to my mother
And you saw me for the first time:
    My face shining out at you,
    Round and red,
    Your inevitable apple.

Watching My Mother Sleep

Hospitals at night
are such deceptive places
and as I watch her sleep
in this strange green light
she looks so young.

And as she sleeps
her right hand opens and closes
as though she is reaching for
something that isn't there.

At her side the machine
is keeping track of her breathing
the way the old grandfather clock
kept track of time.

She told me once that
when I was born she could
feel my heartbeat leaving her
and for a moment there was
such a terrible emptiness inside

she said she knew what
it must feel like to die.
Why is it one of us is always
leaving or just coming back
to say good-bye?

Her sleep now is so quiet
it's deceiving and between
each breath is such an emptiness
that every time I wonder
if she has died

or is this the emptiness
of my birth she's remembering
or could it be that I'm
remembering my own:

waking to find my mother
in her twilight sleep
weeping because I'm gone.

My Grandmother's Eighty-sixth Birthday

The cake at my grandmother's birthday party
was chocolate with white icing which is her
favorite.

Although she could not blow out all the
candles, she said her wish had already
come true.

Mother Mercy

She is the spider woman of my nightmares,
        said to be a cross between myself,
        my mother, and the nun at the hospital
        who wrapped her black arms around me
        and held me.

She is the one who weaves her way down the
        dark hall to find me,

        whose shadow creeps over me while
        I sleep,

        whose thin voice unwinds like
        a thread.

She is the one who tends me with her silent
        hands,

        touches me with her dark fingers.

She is the only one who hears me calling
        "help me, help me."

She is the only one who really cares.

Implications and Remains

I

He gave me hot-chocolate for breakfast
And put raisins in my oatmeal.
I was his princess-child
But he never made any promises.

II

We ate watermelon on the beaches
Until I went away to school
He sent me extra money every month
Still hoping actions speak louder than words.

III

I'm sure that after years of uncommunication
He thinks I have forgotten him,
Not knowing that still
I put honey in my tea.

My Grandfather's Garden

Every spring my grandfather
takes his hoe and spade
and packages of seeds
and goes into the yard
to plant his garden.

All summer he tends
the fragile stems
watching them as a new father
watches for his child's breathing
clearing the ground for them
aware of each new leaf and bud.

And after a while
it is time for the asparagus
to be cut and strawberries
to be brought in and
beans and peppers and rhubarb
fill the pantry shelves.

And cucumbers and cabbages
are ready to be sliced
and put in crocks of brine
in the cellar and all
the green tomatoes are lined up
along the kitchen window sill.

But this year things have not
been growing quite as well
and even after dinner
my grandfather works in his garden
sitting between the frail tomato plants
fingering the earth
his hands pale and wrinkled
as delicate as lettuce.

The Magi

There are no stars tonight
except for the flickering of street lights
on the flakes of snow.
And now the house has settled
under the quiet weight of evening.

Upstairs my grandfather and my nephew
are sleeping side by side in the same room.
Light from the open door falls between them.
Each in a kind of half sleep
they fall into each other's dreams:
   a child's first Christmas
   an old man's last.

Meanwhile my grandmother is in the kitchen
folding baby clothes, humming the old lullaby
about the angel with six wings
and eyes that never sleep.

Life After Death

(for Burnett, 1945–1971)

*Some of us die young
because we want to know
everything.*

I

You lived too soon.
If you had waited,
if you had slowed down
for a moment
I might have caught up with you.

Instead, I was always arriving
just as you were ready to leave.
Our few moments together
were always spent saying good-bye.

But that summer our timing was off.
I arrived but you were
already gone.

I looked for you
among the faces at the airport
but you were not there.

I went back to the places
where we used to meet
but you were not there.

I've heard that
when a person dies
he sees his whole life
pass before him.

Is that true? Did you
see me in that last moment?
Was I there?

II

The children we never had
are dying inside me.
Their faces are moons
on dark water.
They drift closer and closer
almost within reach.

Their eyes float open
milk white and blind.
They dream of waking.
I dream of holding them
asleep in my arms.

I hear their heartbeats
like the echo in seashells
deep inside me. For a moment
I could almost feel them
their feet and elbows nudging me
their small bodies turning.

Now they are sinking
deeper and deeper into me
holding their twisted life lines
in their hands, attached
to nothing.

Not even wreckage
floats on the dark water.
Not even the moon.

III

You knew your life was suicide
    but it didn't stop you.

You knew too much.

You knew the last step would be the hardest
    the one where there is nothing under
    your foot.

You knew the rest would come easily.

You knew the fall would justify the climb.

You knew too much.

You knew too many languages.

You knew there were no words
    for what had to be said.

You knew your bones spread over the rocks
    would say enough.

You knew your past would always hold onto you.

You knew how to let go.

You knew too much.

But you wanted to know everything.

IV

The things I know:
      how the living go on living
      and how the dead go on living with them

So that in a forest
      even a dead tree casts a shadow
      and the leaves fall one by one
      and the branches break in the wind
      and the bark peels off slowly
      and the trunk cracks
      and the rain seeps in through the cracks
      and the trunk falls to the ground
      and the moss covers it

      and in the spring the rabbits find it
      and build their nest inside
      and have their young
      and their young will live safely
      inside the dead tree
So that nothing is wasted in nature
      or in love.

 *II*

Neither the First War Poem Nor the Last

If it is a monument
    it stands alone
    in the middle of a town square
    now deserted.

The people are elsewhere
    working, shopping, in school.

No one gathers here anymore—
    the wood benches have fallen apart.

No one knows how long the monument
    has been here.

There is no plaque with any information.

It is just a statue of a soldier weeping
    holding his helmet in his hand.

No one knows who the soldier is.

No one remembers why the monument
    was built.

He is probably not a hero
    probably no one in particular
    neither the first soldier
    nor the last.

My Great-grandmother's Wristwatch

My great-grandmother's wristwatch still keeps
perfect time. My mother said, as far as she can
remember, it's always kept perfect time, when her
grandmother had it, when her mother had it, and when
she had it. But a few years ago it stopped and none
of the jewelers she took it to could fix it. They
said it was too old and they didn't have parts for
it. My mother saved it for sentimental value and
it sat around the house for a couple of years.

Then she gave it to me because I needed a watch and
she said I could have it if I could get it fixed.
Most jewelers wouldn't even look at it, it was so
old. Finally in New York I found a watchmaker who
specialized in antiques. He cleaned and polished
my great-grandmother's watch and now it looks as
good as new. He said it's a fine piece of machinery.
He said it just needed some minor adjustments. He
said it works perfectly. He said it should last
another lifetime.

**Concerning the Gold Fountain Pen Sent to Me by
My Father on My Twenty-first Birthday with a
Note Congratulating Me on My New Independence**

Daddy: I am returning the pen you sent and with
it all affiliated responsibilities. I don't want
to sign my own checks, leases, legal documents. I
don't want to graduate this June. I don't want to
get a job. I don't mind being declared a dependent.
It does not make me feel inferior.

I am really quite happy with my life as it is now
and I think it would be foolish to make any unneces-
sary changes. I do appreciate, however, your feeling
of confidence in me and your faith that I am capable
of taking on these new responsibilities; and I do
not mean to imply that you were mistaken about me.
I simply want to explain that I think you are being
a bit hasty in your judgement. There is no need to
rush the future; it will come soon enough.

Nor do I wish you to be offended by the fact that I
am returning the pen. This gesture is not meant to
imply that you are in any way inadequate as a father
or were unsuccessful at preparing me for my adult
life. On the contrary, you have been an ideal father
and consequently I am very happy to continue with our
usual relationship.

Love, as always,

Your little girl

Hanging On

After we have been introduced we shake hands
and we shake hands for a long time.

Your hand is bigger than mine but we
learn to compensate. My hand has a
tendency to get nervous and shake vio-
lently but your hand is very reassuring.
Eventually we have the perfect handshake.

Time passes and we continue shaking hands.
We both feel it is very natural and
very beautiful and both of us are at
ease. Neither of us can remember what
our hands did before they met.

My hand begins to daydream about the
future, about shaking hands forever
and the feeling of security.

Suddenly your hand becomes cold and
very limp. My hand does not understand
what has happened and tries frantically
to revive you. When there is no response
my hand recognizes that your hand is dead.

Other hands crowd around trying to console
me but I refuse to let go. I learn to
shelter your hand to keep it warm. I
learn to support your hand to keep it
from slipping away. Eventually I learn
to compensate for everything.

Love Poem for a Dead Man

I return to the scene of the accident
    the way a thief returns
    to the scene of the crime
    looking for something
    he may have left behind

    the way a detective returns
    to the scene of the crime
    looking for answers

    the way the witnesses return
    to the scene of the crime
    to refresh their memories.

I return each day to the scene of the accident
    as though I am returning
    to the scene of a crime

    not knowing what it was
    that I stole from you
    and not being able
    to return it.

The Field Where You Lost Your Mother

The field where you lost your mother
is the same field where you lost
your tricycle years ago.

She told you never to play there
where you couldn't be seen
above the tall grass. But the grass
kept waving to you.

And one day it opened and invited
you inside and you rode in
on your tricycle, your fists tight
on the handlebars and your feet
grinding the wheels into the soft mud.

And each stem moved aside
as you passed by it and
each door opened just as
you arrived.

And when you saw the butterfly
dipping down between the stalks
you had to follow, leaving
your tricycle wedged into
the roots of grass.

And when the butterfly was gone
the field closed in around you
and the tall stems brushed against
your eyes. And you tried to
retrace your steps but you
couldn't find them.

And for years every day you
went back searching through the
tall grass for your tricycle.

So when you came home and
saw your father weeping
and he told you
you had lost your mother,
you knew where to look for her:

In the field
where you knew you would not
find her.

The Hub of the Universe

The hub of the universe is here
      in the laundry room
deep in the heart of the basement
with the rattles and bangs of the
      washing machines
and the steady hum of the dryers.

Here in the laundry room
things are made clean again;
the past forgotten. Here,
the grime of life is removed.

Sheets and towels are made sweet
      again,
the grass stains of childhood
      are washed away,
and all the articles of living
are refreshed, renewed,

but not reborn: the old keep
      getting older,
the colors fade, the whites turn
      grey or yellow;
frayed cuffs go on wearing away
      thread by thread;
buttons fall off and are lost forever.

Here, the true softness of the fabric
      is revealed
and the clothes, clean and innocent,
are sent back into the world
to be worn again.

The Whole Truth

It's true what they say
    about little girls being
    in love with their fathers.
It's true and you don't forget

even when you're grown and
    haven't been home for years
or when you look at your father
    and see an old man.

And it's true that no matter
    how happy you are now
    or how far away
you still dream of going back

remembering as far back
    as you can remember
how he looked then
    how lean and agile
    how young

and you remember falling
    asleep in his lap
and you remember him sitting
    on the edge of your bed
    reading you stories

and you remember pretending
    to be asleep as he
    stood there watching you
resting his large hand
    on your forehead and
    smoothing back your hair.

And you can remember but
        you can never go back again
and even if you could
        it wouldn't be the same
        you'd want more now

and you wouldn't be satisfied
        with a simple hand
        on the forehead
or to sit quietly on his lap
        you'd want more

and you couldn't just lie there
        pretending to sleep
you would have to reach out
        and touch his forehead
        and push the hair back
        out of his eyes

and you couldn't stop there
        wanting him to lie down
        next to you
wanting your face next to his
        on the tiny pillow.

But you can't go back again
        so you find another man
with the same agile body
        and a similar smile

and sleeping next to him
        at night
when he turns to kiss you
        and you reach out to him
        and his whole body
        is next to you

you know it's true
          that little girls were
          meant to grow up
and women were meant
          to fall in love

because you learn so much
          when you're young
and you don't forget.

My Mother's Nightmares

She has nightmares now
although she never used to
and sometimes when I'm there
I hear her cry out in her sleep
sometimes calling me by name
but when she wakes
she says she can't remember
what she's dreamed.

She used to dream that
both of us were drowning.
She could hear me crying
calling out her name.
She searches for me in the
dark water until it's too late
even to save herself.

I seem to have outgrown my nightmares
but many times at night I can't sleep
and I lie there in the dark
and listen for my mother's voice
as we call out to each other
each of us in our distant dreams.

An Afternoon of Painting

And the artist, carrying
his watercolor, walks
home in the rain.

At the Point of Waking

At the point of waking, as at no other time,
it is possible to hold dreams. And even then,
it is only for a few seconds: the moment when
you are awake enough to realize you are still
asleep. And whatever dream is with you, for
that one moment, becomes tangible. You are
able to touch it, stroke it, like a tame animal
asleep in your lap. And you can feel the soft-
ness of his fur and the gradualness of his move-
ments as he wakes slowly, stretching each paw
out in front of him, licking the darkness from
his whiskers, before he leaps away from you,
taking your warmth with him, and leaving his
with you.

The Tomb of the Unborn Soldier

It is a way of life for these women
who go each day to the cemeteries
carrying flowers and who return
empty handed.

I Rarely Dream of Orpheus

There is no sunlight here
                    beneath these trees.
Only the shadows are mute enough
to strum through my bones—
                    Is that me, weeping?
Or is that you, calling my name?

Following the silence
                    you will find me here,
wrapped in your absence as the
morning is shrouded in dreams.
                    Can you wake me?
Or can I persuade you to sleep?

Here where the darkness flows
                    like a river between us,
I do not know whose reflection I see
drifting backwards; nor can I tell
                    which shore is darker.
Which one of us is dead?

Spring Cleaning

All morning
I have been pulling
skeletons out of the closet
the old bones that
keep me awake at night
the old faces I see
in my dreams.

But in the closet
there are only old letters
old clothes that don't fit
boxes of souvenirs
postcards of favorite places
Dust stirs in the corners
like a secret heart
trying to beat again.

Wreckage from an old war
I sit like a widow
sifting through it
touching the skeletons
for the last time.
It is spring and
time to let go of them
let the closet billow
with fresh air.

And if it's true
that the past is
always with us
then let it be
invisible as an angel.
But first I must
bury these old bones.

 *III*

Separation

My shadow is leaving me.
It has rejected my solidness.
It says I am too definitive;
I lack ambiguity.
It is tired of my pedestrian ways.

I have offered it stability
but it wants to be free,
feathery, graceful as smoke,
to rise and drift, to dance,
most of all, to dance, unencumbered,
unrestrained by the bulk of my
heaviness.

I have tried to warn it
of the dangers of groundlessness
but it will not listen.

Poor shadow.
When I walk into a forest
I will find shreds of it
in all the trees.

The Whole of It

I am as resilient as a robin's egg
falling out of the nest
twenty feet above ground.

My one salvation
is the little boy across the street
who collects odds and ends.

Is Here

Everything I own is here

these books
these chairs
this table

when I reach out for them
they meet my touch

they help support me
they bear up under my weight
they bend to my will

they offer me encouragement
at ease in my presence
in this room

none of us have to be here
and yet all of us are

and all of us have been around
long enough to know it is best

to be firm and silent
and accept the way
each thing fits in.

My Shadow

My shadow is lying on top of me
       like a lover
whispering sweet nothings in my ear.

He devotes himself to me entirely,
       and day after day,
he never lets me out of his sight.

My shadow sleeps with one eye open;
       the other eye is always on me.

He is afraid I will slip away from him
       during the night,
and he would die without me.

He is afraid to be alone, and also
       he is afraid of the dark.
He needs me, he begs me to stay.

He knows I hate him. I hate
       the way he clings to me.
He refuses to leave me alone.

He is smudged across my life
       like watery, indelible ink.
He is a black mark against me.

If I could kill him, I would;
       I've tried hundreds of times
and I know it is hopeless.

Always he reappears; at night he
        haunts me, waking me,
trembling and cold.

And all night I feel his tears
        dripping down my face.
And he lies awake, saying,

        Hold me, hold me.
And I lie awake, saying,
        I can't.

The Apple

You gave me your heart
like a polished apple
and being young
I bit into it

letting my teeth
pierce the tight skin
deep into the flesh
while the juices
ran down between
my fingers.

But now I'm not sure
what fruit it is
that I've eaten
or from what tree

or why suddenly
neither one of us
is quite as young.

The Dying Tree

It is obvious that the tree is dying.

At first, when it began to grow sideways,
        I thought perhaps that it was just
        afraid of heights.
But when it began to grow more down than out,
        I realized it had taken a turn for the
        worse.

The question is:
        Should I put myself in a position to
        support this tree?

It would, of course, be difficult and require
        a great deal of time.
And I would have to withstand great extremes
        of heat and cold, as well as minor
        inconveniences of hunger, mosquitoes,
        and curious squirrels.
It would be a full-time occupation with
        no time for vacations or coffee-breaks.
And mechanically it would require a high
        degree of concentration and skill:
                I could stand on the top rung of
                a ladder, lean against the trunk,
                and stretch out each arm to support
                a limb.
It would be a great sacrifice.

But how do you say no to a dying tree?

Souvenir

Not in bitterness
I cross your name off the list
and my name off the list
and since they were the only two
      names on the list
I crumple up the piece of paper
and give it to you as a token
      of our separation together.

Death

Time stops.
At last it is quiet enough
for me to go to sleep.

Time starts again,
I go on sleeping.

Dust

The doctor puts his stethoscope to my forehead
and hears nothing. "Dead" he reports.

"Dead whether you know it or not—
you can tell by the eyes aimed inward,
the breathing inaudibly still. Doomed
from the start. It was only a matter of time."

And he pulls the sheet over my face and leaves.
When he's gone, I push the sheet away
and open my eyes to the sterile morning.

Odd, to be alone in the room with a body.
(Look, my shroud has flowers on the cuff!)
I reach over to see what my hand feels like—
I should have known—my hand is like ice.

"I'm sorry. I'm truly sorry."
I close my eyes again and pretend
not to breathe. It is hopeless.

Indian Giver

Crossing the desert I met an Indian selling
authentic headdresses imported from South
West Utah at special discount prices and he
wanted to sell me one but I said I didn't
have any money but he said I could pay him
by writing him a poem but I said I really
didn't need a headdress and he said he didn't
really need a poem which seemed like a fair
exchange so I scribbled something in the sand
which he couldn't understand but he liked my
handwriting so he gave me the headdress which
turned out to be made in Japan so we said
good-bye and I walked away with dirty finger-
nails and feathers coming out of my ears.

Night Song

And when she
woke suddenly
in the empty room
crying mother, mother,

the moon, watching
at a distance, rose
over her bed
and stayed there
until she was
asleep.

January

It is January again
and it is time to begin
a new year again

because the old year is over
and it is January again
and time to begin again
and in a year this year
will end and it will be
time to begin again
because it will be January
again but this is only
the beginning.

Meanwhile
the snow continues
and January goes on
for an interminably
long time.

Body Count

The corpses are laid out
like cucumbers in the grocery window.
        Four hundred eighty-three
        Four hundred eighty-four
It has taken all morning to get this far.
        Four hundred eighty-five

If I
were dead
        would I recognize my body?
Would I hesitate momentarily
        knowing it was me?
Perhaps I could identify it
        by the little scar on my abdomen
        or a scattering of freckles
        in some recognizable design.
Or perhaps I would just know,
        instinct would tell me
        and draw me closer and closer
        to that one body.
Perhaps I would take it in my arms
        like a mourning mother
        or a widow.
Or perhaps, in anger, I would
        slash it open even more
        trying to deface it
        beyond all recognition.
Or perhaps I would hesitate
        just long enough
        and then pass quickly by
        hoping no one else would notice
        or make any connection
        between it and me.

Or perhaps I would not even notice at all.
Perhaps my mind would be too full of numbers
     to take the time to look.
Perhaps I would say
     Four hundred eighty-six
And just walk by.

A Fine Afternoon for Flying Kites

They have fallen asleep with their hats on
under the trees. It is still cold and their
breath blooms above their mouths like white
flowers which they inhale repeatedly. They
are not as young as they used to be.

The kite lying beside them in the grass pulls
restlessly towards the wind the way an old
dog dreams of chasing rabbits.

If they wake now it is still light enough
to send the kite up one last time in a final
burst of energy and freedom.

If they sleep until dark, they will probably
send the kite up anyway, letting it follow
them home like a distant star.

IV

The Two-headed Calf

Tomorrow when the farm boys find this
freak of nature, they will wrap his body
in newspaper and carry him to the museum.

But tonight he is alive and in the north
field with his mother. It is a perfect
summer evening: the moon rising over
the orchard, the wind in the grass.
And as he stares into the sky, there
are twice as many stars as usual.

The Secret

There is a secret to it—how a frog egg becomes a
frog. It is a secret that only frogs know and
they pass this knowledge on from generation to
generation, improving it, changing it slightly
over the millions of years, but never losing the
fundamental knowledge of how to become a frog.

Humans now understand how this secret is handed
down through the generations. All the necessary
information is carried on the chromosomes of each
cell of every frog, from parent to child and to
that child's children.

But although humans understand how the secret is
passed along, only the frogs know what the secret
is.

The Friends

1. The catalyst begins a reaction or a chain of
   reactions which may be endless, but after the
   first reaction the catalyst is of no importance.

2. The catalyst has provided the energy for a reaction
   to occur in which the element reacting has been
   changed. Although originally this element may have
   been inert and unable to react with other elements,
   because of this first initial reaction, the element
   has been changed and is now able to react and respond
   without the presence of a catalyst.

3. The catalyst, however, begins only the initial
   reaction. It then has no further effect on the
   element. Although the reaction affects the element,
   the catalyst itself remains unchanged.

4. The catalyst begins a reaction or a chain of
   reactions which may be endless, but after the
   first reaction the catalyst is of no importance.

A Toast to the Alchemists

Alchemists,
you were right, it is
possible.
We have the proof now.
There are equations.

If you could come back
for a day, if you could
conjure yourself into
this chemistry classroom,
if you could read the
textbook or watch the
professor writing the
answers on the board . . .

Alchemists,
you would see that you
were right, even though
you didn't know about
alpha and beta radiation,
even though you didn't
understand isotopes,
you knew it was possible,
that some elements can
change into other elements,
that transmutation can
occur.

Alchemists,
there is proof now that
it is possible, although
each new element, having
a brief half-life, would
keep changing into other
things.

Alchemists,
you were right, you can
make anything, anything,
uranium, plutonium, tel-
lurium, mercury, copper,
cobalt, platinum, silver,
and gold, you can make
gold, an isotope so
radioactive it would
sparkle before your eyes.

Alchemists,
you were right.
It is magic.

Examination

The grass is green. Do you know why?
The sky is blue.   Do you know why?
Can you tell me what life is?

You mean you don't know?
You mean you only have vague ideas?
What do you mean it's not important?

Aren't you interested in the scientific
        approach to life?
Wouldn't you like to prove your abstract
        hypotheses, to find evidence for your
        reasonable conclusions?

Scientists explain that the grass is green
        because of a substance called chlorophyll,
        from the Greek words "chloro" and "phyll"
        meaning "green leaf."
They say the sky is blue because of reflections.

Have you ever thought seriously about reflections?
When you look in a mirror do you know what you see?
Move closer to it.
Look into each eye like the aperture of a microscope.
Can you bring it into focus?
Can you identify what you see?
Is it moving?
Can you see it grow?
Is it trying to divide?
Is it empty?
Is it sucking in what's around it?

Is it still moving?
Is it moving towards something?
Is it moving away from something?
Is it near the edge?
Has it stopped moving?
Do you know why?
Is it watching you?
Do you know what it sees?
Can you identify what it sees?
Can you ask it to describe what it sees?
Can you ask it to explain its answers?
Can you ask it to explain other answers?
Can you ask it to explain why the grass is green?
Can you understand its answer?
Do you speak the same language?

Snow

Each flake of snow
so separate
so distinct

yet in the morning
the hillside is a
solid field of white.

Infinity

Infinity is what you don't understand
      like the number of stars, for example.

You say there is an infinite number of stars
      only because you haven't counted them.

      (Better to plead infinity than ignorance.)

But the stars can be counted
      and grains of sand can be counted
      and blades of grass can be counted
      flakes of snow can be counted
      drops of water in the sea can be counted
      molecules in the universe can be counted
      atoms and electrons can be counted
      photons can be counted . . .

Only what you don't know is infinite.

Egg and Sperm

She waits for him
in the dark tunnels of love
listening for voices.

A red moon is just rising
above the blood line
on the horizon. A red
sun disappearing is
staining the sky pink.

Somewhere in the distance
the sound of waves
like heavy breathing. It is
a perfect night for love
but no one is there.

Is this the place?
Is this . . . ? Is it always
waiting?

She sings a few songs
to herself to pass the time.
What if it's too late?
Who are we waiting for
in these empty nights?

She dozes and wakes suddenly
thinking she's heard voices
or has she only dreamed them?

Someone has come to her.
Someone is touching her.
He leans against her and she
circles him with her arms.
She opens for him: he
moves inside.

And for that moment they are
so much a part of each other
that the whole universe
must readjust itself
around them.

Differences

Of the six kernels of corn I planted,
only four sprouted, and of those four,
only two survived, and of those two,
one is taller.

Seeing a Dog in the Rain

It is raining and there is a dog lying
in the gutter and the gutter is filling
with water because the sewer is clogged.

If the dog were alive he would be drowning
but as it is, the water is simply stroking
his fur.

Coming Home

You wanted to come home
for your favorite season
but you're too late.
Only the tight fists of apples
still cling to the trees.

And as you stand in the back yard
helping your father rake
the leaves out from between
the apple trees,
it is almost winter.

The swallows have already
gathered up their shadows
and moved south
and the cardinals,
perched in the top branches,
are listening for snow.

With each stroke of the rake
you uncover more leaves,
mushrooms, soft decaying apples,
heaping them into the wheelbarrow
like debris.

Your father has kept the fire burning.
You pile on more leaves and
both of you watch the smoke rise
like the shadow of birds
leaving.

You've come home unprepared
for this new season
the way a worm falls asleep
beside an apple blossom
and wakes up deep in the fruit.